CALORIES & WEIGHT:
The USDA Pocket Guide

This publication is part of ''Eating Right...The Dietary Guidelines Way,'' USDA's ongoing nutrition education program to help consumers put the Dietary Guidelines into practice.

Maintain Desirable Weight...is one of seven Dietary Guidelines recommended by the U.S. Departments of Agriculture and of Health and Human Services. Choosing a good diet is a balancing act. The goal is to eat a variety of foods that supply the nutrients and fiber you need, but not too many calories or too much fat, cholesterol, sugar, sodium, or alcohol. This bulletin is about calories and your weight. Excess weight or obesity is harmful to your health and may shorten your life. It is associated with high blood pressure, heart disease, the most common type of diabetes, certain cancers, and many other types of ill health.

Weight...Is Yours "Right" for You?

Weight range charts (see page 3) can help you decide whether you have a weight problem, but they don't tell the whole story. Some people weigh more than the chart shows, but their excess weight is primarily muscle. Overweight is only a problem if the excess pounds are fat. Are your excess pounds fat? Looking in the mirror or pinching a fold of skin at the back of your upper arm are quick tests. If you can pinch more than an inch, your excess weight probably comes from fat.

Desirable Body Weight Ranges for Adults

Height without shoes	Weight without clothes	
	Men (pounds)	Women (pounds)
4'10"		92-121
4'11"		95-124
5'0"		98-127
5'1"	105-134	101-130
5'2"	108-137	104-134
5'3"	111-141	107-138
5'4"	114-145	110-142
5'5"	117-149	114-146
5'6"	121-154	118-150
5'7"	125-159	122-154
5'8"	129-163	126-159
5'9"	133-167	130-164
5'10"	137-172	134-169
5'11"	141-177	
6'0"	145-182	
6'1"	149-187	
6'2"	153-192	
6'3"	157-197	

NOTE: For women 18-25 years of age, subtract 1 pound for each year under 25.

SOURCE: Adapted from the 1959 Metropolitan Desirable Weight Table.

Taking the Mystery Out of Calories

What is a calorie? A calorie is a measure of energy, the capacity to do work. Science defines the calorie as the amount of energy required to raise the temperature of 1 gram of water by 1 degree Celsius. In the laboratory, the calories in a food are determined by measuring the amount in 1,000-calorie units called kilocalories. But in everyday language this term has been shortened to just "calorie" when the amount of energy in food is described. Thus, the 165-calorie bagel (page 18) is really 165 kilocalories.

How many calories do you need? Your body needs energy for growth, maintenance, and physical activity. The energy (calorie) intake suggested by the Food and Nutrition Board of the National Research Council for women 25 to 50 years of age who are 5 feet 4 inches tall and weigh 138 pounds is 2,200 calories. For men that age who are 5 feet 10 inches tall and 174 pounds, it's 2,900 calories. These calorie levels are for women and men of the reference height and weight engaged in light to moderate activity. The number of calories you need depends on your height and weight as well as your age, body size, physical condition, and physical activity. Younger adults require more calories than older adults. Active people require more calories than inactive people. When the food you eat provides more calories than your body needs, the excess calories are stored as fat and you gain weight.

Do all calories count? Yes...all calories count, regardless of the food they come from. But some foods have more calories than others. Most foods are mixtures of water, protein, carbohydrate, and fat. The number of calories in a food depends on how much of each of these is present. Proteins and carbohydrates have about 4 calories per gram while fats have about 9. Water has no calories. Alcohol also provides calories, about 7 per gram.

Is there a secret to losing weight? Whether you have 5 pounds or 20 pounds to lose, the only way you can lose weight is to consistently eat foods containing fewer calories than your body needs and uses. This means that you must either select foods containing fewer calories than you normally eat or you must increase your activity—preferably both. An average loss of 1 or 2 pounds a week is about right. Do not try to lose weight too rapidly.

Diet Cautions

Diet fads—Be suspicious of diet gimmicks and fad diets that promise wonders. They can be dangerous. Some are appealing because they promise quick and easy weight loss, but unless a diet is balanced nutritionally—as many fad diets are not—it can be harmful if followed over a period of time. Diets that encourage little or no eating and diets that promote heavy eating of one kind of food can cause health problems. Some people have developed kidney problems, disturbing psychological changes, and other complications while following these diets.

You can be too thin. Being overweight is not advisable—but neither is being much **below** your desirable weight. Losing too much weight can cause health problems. Anorexia nervosa and bulimia are serious eating disorders. Persons with these disorders usually think they look fat (even though they may be thin) and have an abnormal fear of being fat. Common traits of persons suffering from anorexia and/or bulimia include bizarre food habits, refusal to eat, binging or gorging followed by vomiting, abuse of laxatives and diuretics, and an extreme urge to exercise. Such practices can result in chronic health problems and even death.

Talk to your doctor if you plan to follow a low-calorie diet for a long time, or an extremely low-calorie diet even for a short time.

Don't Forget Exercise

Cutting calorie intake is one way to shed pounds—but the best approach is to decrease calories (particularly calories from fat and sugar) **and** increase physical activity. Exercise burns calories and improves overall fitness as you lose weight. It can also help relieve stress that may lead to overeating.

Don't feel that you have to be an athlete to make physical activity count. In fact, it's best to make slow, steady increases in your activity level. There are many ways to increase the activity level in your daily routine: walk or bicycle instead of driving, use the stairs instead of the elevator, stand rather than sit.

The number of calories burned depends on the vigor of the activity (running burns more than walking), length of the activity (the longer the activity continues, the more calories burned), and your weight (a heavier person uses more calories than a lighter person for the same activity). Remember that even small changes in activity level can make a difference over time.

Caution: Before you start an exercise or sports program, check with your doctor to help you decide what activity is best for your age and general physical condition.

Foods To Include in a Healthy Weight Loss Plan

A healthy weight loss plan includes a diet made up of a variety of foods. More than 40 nutrients are important for good health. No one food contains all of these nutrients in the amounts needed. Thus, you need different kinds of foods in your diet. A healthy weight loss plan counts on the lower calorie choices from these different kinds of foods. To help you plan a varied diet, we've grouped foods by the nutrients they contain:

- Breads, cereals, and other grain products
- Fruits
- Vegetables
- Meat, poultry, fish, and alternates (eggs, dry beans, and nuts)
- Milk, yogurt, and cheese

A varied diet contains servings from each of these groups daily. The nutrient contribution of each of these food groups is described on the next several pages. The foods listed in the Calorie Table are organized into these groups so you can compare calories for similar foods more easily. We've also included information on the calories in fats, sweets, and beverages, as well as items that are combinations of foods in several groups—mixed main dishes and fast food entrees; soups; and desserts, snack foods, and candy.

Breads, cereals, and other grain products...
Most of these foods are not high in calories, but some with added sugars and fats are. Check pages 18 to 28 for examples. Of course, the spreads, such as margarine and jelly, that are used on breads and crackers add calories. So does the sugar added to cereals. Both whole-grain and enriched breads and cereals provide starch, thiamin, riboflavin, niacin, and iron. Whole grains are also good sources of fiber and provide folate (folacin, folic acid), magnesium, and zinc. Choose at least six servings of grain products every day including some whole grains. Many of these

foods are not high in calories. A serving is one slice of bread; a half hamburger bun or english muffin; a small roll, biscuit, or muffin; three or four small or two large crackers; ½ cup of cooked cereal, rice, or pasta; or 1 ounce of ready-to-eat breakfast cereal.

Fruits...
Fruits are generally low in calories, contain dietary fiber, and provide vitamins and minerals. Citrus fruits (oranges and grapefruit), melons, and berries are excellent sources of vitamin C. Deep-yellow fruits—such as apricots and cantaloups—are high in vitamin A. All of these fruits and others provide additional nutrients such as folate (folacin, folic acid), potassium, and magnesium. Include at least two servings of fruit every day. Fruits and fruit juices are listed on pages 28 to 37. Sweetened fruits provide extra calories. A serving is a piece of whole fruit, such as an apple, banana, or orange; a grapefruit half; a melon wedge; ¾ cup of juice; ½ cup of berries or ½ cup of cooked or canned fruit; or ¼ cup of dried fruit.

Vegetables...

Vegetables, like fruits, are generally low in calories and are sources of dietary fiber and many vitamins and minerals. However, putting margarine or butter on vegetables or cooking greens with fatty meats makes the calories go up. Dark-green vegetables, such as spinach and broccoli, provide vitamin C, riboflavin, folate (folacin, folic acid), calcium, and magnesium. These, along with deep-yellow vegetables, such as carrots, are excellent sources of vitamin A in the form of carotenes. Starchy vegetables, such as potatoes and green peas, contribute starch as well as potassium. Dry beans and peas (legumes) are also a source of these nutrients as well as folate, iron, phosphorus, magnesium, and protein. Legumes can be used as a starchy vegetable as well as an alternate to meat. Other vegetables that make important nutrient contributions include cauliflower, tomatoes, asparagus, and cabbage. You need at least three servings of vegetables every day and dark-green vegetables and cooked dry beans and peas several times a week. Vegetables are listed on pages 37 to 46 and legumes on pages 59 to 60. A serving is ½ cup of cooked or chopped raw vegetables or 1 cup of leafy raw vegetables, such as lettuce or spinach.

Meat, poultry, fish, and alternates...
The foods in this group are important sources of protein, niacin, vitamins B-6 and B-12, iron, phosphorus, and zinc. Meat, poultry, and fish also provide fat and cholesterol, but you can select and prepare items from this group so that the amount of fat is quite modest. Choose lean cuts of meat; trim visible fat from meat; remove the skin from chicken; and prepare by baking or broiling instead of frying. The listing on pages 46 to 58 shows how different kinds and forms of the foods in this group can affect calorie content. Include two to three servings (a total of 5 to 7 ounces) per day of lean meat, poultry, fish, or the alternates discussed below.

Eggs can be used as an alternate to lean meat, poultry, and fish. Egg yolks are high in cholesterol, but they are also a source of minerals and other nutrients. Count one egg as 1 ounce of meat. Dry beans and peas (legumes) and various nuts and seeds can also be used as alternates. Count ½ cup of cooked dry beans or peas or ¼ cup of nuts as 1 ounce of meat. The protein, vitamin, and mineral content of legumes and nuts are similar to those of meat, but they do not contain vitamin B-12. Beans and peas contain carbohydrates and, with the exception of soybeans, are lower in fat than lean meat. Nuts and seeds are much higher in fat and calories than lean meat. Eggs, dry beans and peas, and nuts and seeds are listed on pages 58 to 62.

Milk, yogurt, and cheese...
Selections from this group differ greatly in calorie content. But the best sources of calcium in the United States are milk, yogurt, and cheese. These foods also provide protein, riboflavin, vitamin B-12, and, if fortified, vitamins A and D. Everyone should include two servings of milk, yogurt, or cheese daily. Teenagers, young adults to 24 years of age, and pregnant and nursing mothers need three servings each day. These foods are listed on pages 62 to 69. A serving is 1 cup of milk, 8 ounces of yogurt, 1½ ounces of natural cheese, or 2 ounces of process cheese.

It's not necessary or a good idea to avoid dairy foods because of a concern about fat and calories. Skim milk, lowfat milk, lowfat yogurt, and lowfat cheese are lower in fat and calories than whole milk, yogurt made with whole milk, and regular cheeses. The amounts of important nutrients that the lowfat products contain is similar to the amounts in higher fat milk products. Sweeteners in fruit yogurt and flavored yogurt also provide extra calories.

Combination foods...

Many foods don't fit into the major food categories because they're combinations of foods from several groups. The Mixed Main Dishes and Fast Food Entrees listed on pages 69 to 73 are examples of these combinations. You can figure out the calories in many other mixed dishes and sandwiches by adding together the calories in their ingredients. Many packaged foods list the number of calories in a serving on the label. When choosing mixed dishes, think about the ingredients they contain and the amount of fat and sugar that have been added. Added fat and sugar means added calories.

Desserts...
The desserts listed on pages 78 to 85 may
provide many of the same nutrients as are
provided by foods in the major food groups.
For example, cake, like bread, contains flour
(from the breads and cereals group) and the
nutrients flour furnishes, and ice cream
contains milk and the nutrients milk furnishes.
But cake and ice cream also contain fat and
sugar and the calories they furnish.

Fats, sweets, and alcoholic beverages...
Foods in this group provide few nutrients
along with their calories. These are "extras"
in the diet—the place to cut calories first. The
calorie contents of these foods are listed on
pages 87 to 99.

Calorie Table

The Calorie Table is organized into sections by food group to make it easier to compare similar types of foods. Sections for foods that are combinations of several food groups— mixed main dishes and fast food entrees; soups; and desserts, snack foods, and candy—are also included. If you're not sure where to find a food, look in the index.

All calorie values in the table were rounded to the nearest 5 calories. The portion sizes listed in the table are in common household units or in pieces of a specified size. All portion sizes are for level measures. To help you judge the size of 3 ounces of meat or poultry, sketches are shown on pages 104 to 106. The portion size shown may not be the amount that you eat. If you choose larger or smaller portions than listed, increase or decrease the calorie counts accordingly. The calorie value for a food item does not include calories from any added fat, sugars, sauce, or dressing unless listed with the item.

BREADS, CEREALS, AND OTHER GRAIN PRODUCTS

Breads   Calories

Bagel, plain, 3-inch diameter, one   **165**

Cracked-wheat, 18-slices-per-pound loaf,
  one slice   **65**

French, 18-slices-per-pound loaf, one slice   **70**

Italian, 18-slices-per-pound loaf, one slice   **70**

Pita, 5¼-inch diameter, one
  white   **125**
  whole-wheat   **115**

Breads-Continued   Calories

Pumpernickel, 18-slices-per-pound loaf,
  one slice   **60**

Raisin, 18-slices-per-pound loaf, one slice   **70**

Rye, 18-slices-per-pound loaf, one slice   **65**

Vienna, 18-slices-per-pound loaf, one slice   **70**

White
  regular-slice, 18-slices-per-pound loaf,
    one slice   **65**
  thin-slice, 22-slices-per-pound loaf,
    one slice   **55**

Whole-wheat, 18-slices-per-pound-loaf,
  one slice   **60**

Rolls

Croissant, 4½ x 4 x 1¾ inches, plain,
one **230**

Dinner, 2½-inch diameter, one **85**

Frankfurter or hamburger, one **130**

Hard, medium, one **155**

Submarine, medium, one-half **145**

Quick Breads, Biscuits, Muffins, and Breakfast Pastries

Calories

Baking powder biscuit, 2-inch
diameter, one
from home recipe **115**
from mix **105**
from refrigerated dough **55**

Banana bread, ½-inch slice of
9- x 5-inch loaf, one   **150**

Coffeecake
  crumb-type, piece 2⅝ x 2 inches,
    one   **100**
  yeast-type, piece ⅛ of 8-inch
    diameter, one   **130**

Cornbread, piece 2½ x 2½ x 1½
inches, one   **160**

Danish pastry, plain, 5-inch diameter,
one   **395**

Doughnuts
  cake-type, plain, 3¼-inch diameter,
    one   **165**
  yeast-leavened, glazed, 3¾-inch
    diameter, one   **245**

English muffin, plain, one   **130**

Muffin, 2⅝-inch diameter, one
blueberry or corn   **165**
bran   **125**

Pancake, plain, 5-inch diameter, one   **90**

Toaster pastry, 4¼ x 3 x ⅜ inches,
one   **210**

Waffle
from mix, 7-inch diameter (about
2¾ ounces), one   **205**
from frozen (about 1½ ounces), one
square   **100**

Breakfast Cereals

Calories

All-Bran®, 1 ounce (about ½ cup) **70**

Bran flakes (40% bran), 1 ounce (about ⅔ cup) **90**

Cheerios®, 1 ounce (about 1 cup) **110**

Corn flakes, 1 ounce (about 1 cup) **110**

Corn (hominy) grits
regular or quick, cooked, ¾ cup **110**
instant, plain, prepared, 1 packet **80**

Corn Pops®, 1 ounce (about 1 cup) **105**

Cream of Wheat®
regular or quick, cooked, ¾ cup **100**
instant, cooked, ¾ cup **130**
Mix'n Eat, plain, prepared, 1 packet **100**

Breakfast Cereals-Continued

Calories

Frosted Flakes®, 1 ounce (about ¾ cup)   **110**

Frosted Mini-Wheats®, 1 ounce (about ½ cup)   **100**

Grape-Nut Flakes®, 1 ounce (about ¾ cup)   **100**

Honey Smacks®, 1 ounce (about ¾ cup)   **105**

Nature Valley® Granola, 1 ounce (about ¼ cup)   **130**

Oatmeal or rolled oats
  regular, quick, or instant, cooked,
    ¾ cup   **110**
  instant, prepared, 1 packet
    plain   **105**
    flavored   **150**

Raisin bran, 1 ounce (about ½ cup)   **85**

Rice Chex®, 1 ounce (about ¾ cup)   **110**

Rice Krispies®, 1 ounce (about 1 cup)   **110**

Shredded wheat, plain
  spoon size, 1 ounce (about ½ cup)   **100**
  large biscuit (about ¾ ounce), one   **85**

Special K®, 1 ounce (about 1-¼ cups)   **110**

Breakfast Cereals-Continued   Calories

Total®, 1 ounce (about ¾ cup)   **100**

Wheaties®, 1 ounce (about 1 cup)   **100**

Pasta and Rice   Calories
(For pasta and rice mixtures, see Mixed Dishes, pages 69-71.)

Macaroni, cooked, plain, ½ cup   **75**

Noodles, cooked, plain, ½ cup   **100**

Rice, cooked, plain, ½ cup
    brown   **115**
    instant   **90**
    white   **110**

Spaghetti, cooked, plain, ½ cup   **75**

Crackers	Calories
Cheese, plain, 1-inch square, 10	**50**
Graham, plain, 2½-inch square, two	**55**
Matzo, 6-inch square, one	**120**
Oyster, 10	**45**
Rye wafers, whole-grain, 1⅞ x 3½ inches, two	**50**
Saltines, 1⅞-inch square, two	**25**
Sandwich-type, peanut butter or cheese filled, two	**80**
Snack-type, round, about 2-inch diameter, two	**30**

Whole-wheat, $1^7/_8$ x $1^5/_8$ inches, two   **30**

FRUITS

Fruits   Calories
*(Calories in cooked and canned fruit include
both fruit and liquid.)*

Apples, raw, medium, one   **80**

Applesauce, canned, ½ cup
  unsweetened   **50**
  sweetened   **95**

Apricots

raw (about 12 per pound), three	**50**
canned, halves, ½ cup	
in juice	**60**
in heavy syrup	**105**
dried halves, cooked, unsweetened, ½ cup	**105**

Avocados

California varieties, 8 ounces each, one-half	**140**
Florida varieties, 16 ounces each, one-half	**245**

Bananas, medium, one   **105**

Blueberries, ½ cup

raw	**40**
frozen	
unsweetened	**40**
sweetened	**95**

Cantaloup, raw
  medium melon, one-fourth   **60**
  cubed, ½ cup   **25**

Cherries, ½ cup
  raw
    sour   **40**
    sweet   **50**
  canned, sweet
    in juice   **70**
    in heavy syrup   **105**

Cranberry sauce, ¼ cup   **105**

Dates, dried, pitted, whole, five   **115**

Fruit cocktail, canned, ½ cup
  in juice   **55**
  in heavy syrup   **90**

Grapefruit
  raw, white, pink, or red
    medium, one-half   **40**
    sections, ½ cup   **35**
  canned, ½ cup
    in juice   **45**
    in light syrup   **75**

Grapes, raw, adherent skin (thompson, red flame, tokay, and emperor), ½ cup   **55**

Honeydew melon, raw
  6- to 7-inch melon, one-eighth   **55**
  cubed, ½ cup   **30**

Kiwifruit, raw, medium, one   **45**

Nectarines, raw, medium, one   **65**

Oranges, raw, medium, one   **60**

Peaches
raw
  whole, medium, one   **40**
  sliced, ½ cup   **35**
canned, ½ cup
  in juice   **55**
  in light syrup   **70**
  in heavy syrup   **95**
dried halves, cooked,
  unsweetened, ½ cup   **100**
frozen, sliced, sweetened, ½ cup   **120**

Pears
raw, medium, one   **100**
canned, ½ cup
  in juice   **60**
  in heavy syrup   **100**

Pineapple
  raw, diced, ½ cup   **40**
  canned
    crushed, tidbits, or chunks, ½ cup
      in juice   **75**
      in heavy syrup   **100**
    slices, two
      in juice   **55**
      in heavy syrup   **75**

Plantains, sliced, cooked, ½ cup   **110**

Plums
  raw, medium, one   **35**
  canned, ½ cup
    in juice   **75**
    in heavy syrup   **115**

Prunes
  dried, cooked, unpitted, ½ cup
    unsweetened   **130**
    sweetened   **150**
  dried, uncooked, five   **85**

Raisins, 1 snack pack, ½ ounce
(1½ tablespoons)   **40**

Raspberries, ½ cup
  raw   **30**
  frozen, sweetened   **130**

Rhubarb, cooked, sweetened, ½ cup   **140**

Strawberries, ½ cup
  raw, sliced   **25**
  frozen, sweetened, sliced   **110**

Tangerines, raw, medium, one	**35**

Watermelon, raw
  wedge or slice (about 1¼-pound piece),
    one
  diced, ½ cup
	90
	25

Fruit Juices   Calories
(A 6-fluid-ounce serving is ¾ cup.)

Apple juice or cider, canned or bottled, 6 fluid ounces	**85**

Apricot nectar, canned, 6 fluid ounces	**105**

Cranberry juice cocktail, bottled, sweetened, 6 fluid ounces	**110**

Grape, 6 fluid ounces
  canned or bottled   **115**
  frozen concentrate, sweetened,
    reconstituted   **95**

Grapefruit, 6 fluid ounces
  fresh   **70**
  canned
    unsweetened   **70**
    sweetened   **85**
  frozen concentrate, unsweetened,
    reconstituted   **75**

Lemon, fresh, canned, or bottled,
  1 tablespoon   **5**

Lime, fresh, canned, or bottled,
  1 tablespoon   **5**

Orange, unsweetened, 6 fluid ounces
   fresh or frozen concentrate, reconstituted **85**
   canned   **80**

Pineapple, canned, unsweetened, 6 fluid
   ounces   **105**

Prune, canned or bottled, 6 fluid
   ounces   **135**

VEGETABLES

Vegetables   Calories
*(Calories are for cooked vegetables
  prepared from raw, canned, or frozen.)*

Alfalfa sprouts, raw, ½ cup   **5**

Artichoke, globe or french, cooked, one
  medium **55**

Asparagus, cooked
  cuts and tips, ½ cup **20**
  medium spears, four **15**

Beans, cooked, ½ cup
  lima (baby or Fordhook) **110**
  snap (green or yellow) **25**

Bean sprouts, mung, ½ cup
  raw **15**
  cooked **30**

Beets, diced or sliced, cooked, ½ cup **25**

Beet greens, chopped, cooked, ½ cup **20**

Broccoli
raw, flowerets, three   **10**
cooked
   chopped, ½ cup   **25**
   5-inch spears, three   **30**

Brussels sprouts, cooked
medium sprouts, four   **35**
½ cup   **30**

Cabbage, ½ cup
raw
   plain, shredded or sliced   **10**
   coleslaw   **70**
cooked, shredded   **15**

Carrots
raw
   7½ x 1⅛ inches, one   **30**
   shredded, ½ cup   **25**
cooked, sliced, ½ cup   **35**

Cauliflower, flowerets
raw, four	**10**
cooked, ½ cup	**20**

Celery
raw, stalk 7½ x 1¼ inches, one	**5**
cooked, diced, ½ cup	**10**

Chives, chopped, raw, 1 tablespoon   **Trace**

Collards, chopped, cooked, ½ cup   **10**

Corn, cooked
on cob, 5-inch ear, one	**80**
kernels, ½ cup	**90**
cream-style, ½ cup	**90**

Cucumbers, raw, six to eight slices   **10**

Eggplant, cubed, cooked, ½ cup	**15**
Endive, pieces for salad, raw, 1 cup	**5**
Kale, chopped, cooked, ½ cup	**20**

Lettuce, raw
  head (iceberg)
    pieces for salad, 1 cup   **5**
    wedge, ⅙ of 6-inch head   **10**
  looseleaf, pieces for salad, 1 cup   **5**

Mushrooms
  raw
    one medium   **5**
    pieces, ½ cup   **10**
  cooked, pieces, ½ cup   **20**

Mustard greens, chopped, cooked, ½ cup **10**

Vegetables-Continued

Okra,
   3-inch pods, fried, eight   **115**
   cooked, sliced, ½ cup   **30**

Onions
   raw, chopped, 2 tablespoons
      young green   **5**
      mature   **5**
   cooked, mature, whole or sliced, ½ cup   **30**

Onion rings, breaded, frozen, prepared,
   2- to 3-inch diameter rings, two   **80**

Peas, green, cooked, ½ cup   **65**

Peppers, sweet, green or red
   raw
      chopped, ½ cup   **20**
      ring, 3-inch diameter, ¼-inch thick,
        one   **Trace**
   cooked, medium, one   **20**

Potatoes

	Calories
au gratin, home-prepared, ½ cup	**175**
baked, 4¾ x 2⅓ inches, flesh and skin, one	**220**
boiled without skin	
2½-inch diameter, one	**105**
diced or sliced, ½ cup	**65**
french-fried (from frozen), 2- to 3½-inch strips, 10	
fried	**160**
oven-heated	**110**
hashed brown (from frozen), ½ cup	**155**
mashed, ½ cup	
from home recipe	
milk added	**80**
milk and fat added	**115**
from dehydrated flakes, milk and fat added	**110**
puffs, oven-heated, 10	**175**
salad, home prepared, ½ cup	**130**
scalloped, home-prepared, ½ cup	**120**

Pumpkin, canned, ½ cup   **30**

Radishes, raw, medium, four	**5**
Sauerkraut, heated, ½ cup	**15**

Spinach
raw, pieces for salad, 1 cup	**5**
cooked, chopped, ½ cup	**20**

Squash, ½ cup
summer, sliced
raw	**10**
cooked	**20**

winter
baked, cubed	**40**
boiled, mashed	**45**

Sweetpotatoes
  baked, 5 x 2 inches, peeled, one   **115**
  candied, piece 2½ x 2 inches, one   **145**
  canned, vacuum or syrup pack, ½ cup
    pieces   **90**
    mashed   **115**

Tomatoes
  raw, medium, one   **25**
  cooked, ½ cup   **25**

Tomato sauce, ½ cup   **35**

Turnips, cubed, ½ cup
  raw   **20**
  cooked   **15**

Turnip greens, chopped, cooked, ½ cup   **15**

Vegetable Juices

Calories

(A 6-fluid-ounce serving is ¾ cup.)

Tomato juice, 6 fluid ounces   **30**

Vegetable juice cocktail, 6 fluid ounces   **35**

MEAT, POULTRY, FISH, AND ALTERNATES

(Serving sizes are cooked, edible part.)

Beef

Calories

Corned beef, canned, 3 ounces
(two slices 4½ x 2½ x ¼ inches)   **210**

Ground beef, broiled, 3 ounces
    regular   **245**
    lean   **230**
    extra lean   **215**

Oven-cooked roast, 3 ounces
  (two slices 4½ x 2½ x ¼ inches)
    relatively fat cuts, such as rib
      lean and fat   **225**
      lean only   **165**
    relatively lean cuts, such as eye of
    round
      lean and fat   **205**
      lean only   **155**

Pot roast, braised or simmered, 3 ounces
  (two slices 4½ x 2½ x ¼ inches)
    relatively fat cuts, such as
    chuck blade
      lean and fat   **330**
      lean only   **235**
    relatively lean cuts, such as
    bottom round
      lean and fat   **225**
      lean only   **190**

Steak, sirloin, broiled, 3 ounces
  (one piece 4½ x 2½ x ½ inches)
    lean and fat   **240**
    lean only   **180**

Veal cutlet, broiled or braised, 3 ounces
  (one piece 4½ x 2½ x ½ inches)   **185**

Lamb   Calories

Ground lamb, broiled, 3 ounces   **305**

Leg, roasted, 3 ounces (two slices
  4½ x 2½ x ¼ inches)
    lean and fat   **235**
    lean only   **160**

Shoulder chop, broiled, 3 ounces of meat
  lean and fat (from about a 5-ounce
    chop, as purchased)   **285**
  lean only (from about a 7-ounce chop,
    as purchased)   **175**

Pork   Calories

Cured
  Ham, canned, heated, lean and fat,
    3 ounces (two slices 4½ x 2½ x ¼
    inches)   **160**
  Ham, cured, roasted, 3 ounces
    (two slices 4½ x 2½ x ¼ inches)
      lean and fat   **205**
      lean only   **135**

Fresh

Loin, roasted, 3 ounces (two slices 4½ x
 2½ x ¼ inches)
    lean and fat   **270**
    lean only   **205**
Loin chop, broiled, 3 ounces of meat
  lean and fat (from about a 5-ounce
    chop, as purchased)   **290**
  lean only (from about a 7-ounce
    chop, as purchased)   **215**
Shoulder (picnic), braised, 3 ounces
 (two slices 4½ x 2½ x ¼ inches)
    lean and fat   **295**
    lean only   **210**

Sausage and Luncheon Meats Calories

Bacon, cooked, slices, three
 (20 slices per pound uncooked)   **140**

Sausage and Luncheon Meats-Continued

Calories

Bologna, 2 ounces (two slices 4½ x ⅛ inches)
    beef and pork   **180**
    chicken or turkey   **115**

Braunschweiger, 2 ounces (two slices 2½ x ⅜ inches)   **205**

Canadian bacon, cooked, two slices (2 ounces uncooked)   **85**

Chicken roll, light meat, 2 ounces (two slices 4½ x ⅛ inches)   **90**

Frankfurter, heated, one (10 per pound unheated)
    beef and pork   **150**
    chicken or turkey   **110**

Ham, chopped, 2 ounces (two slices 4 x 4
  inches) **140**

Ham, boiled, 2 ounces (two slices 6¼
  x 4 inches)
    regular **90**
    extra lean **75**

Pork sausage
  bulk, cooked, one patty (about 2 ounces
    uncooked) **100**
  link, cooked, two links 4 x ⅞ inches
    (2 ounces uncooked) **95**

Salami, 2 ounces (two slices 4½ x ⅛
  inches) **140**

Vienna sausage, canned, sausages 2 x $^7/_8$
   inches, three (about 1¾ ounces)   **135**

Organ Meats   Calories

Beef liver, fried, 3 ounces (one piece
   6½ x 2$^3/_8$ x $^3/_8$ inches)   **185**

Chicken liver, cooked
   one liver   **45**
   3 ounces (about four livers)   **195**

Chicken
  fried
    breast half, one medium
      meat only   **160**
      flour-coated, meat and skin   **215**
      batter-dipped or breaded, meat
        and skin   **365**
    drumstick, one medium
      meat only   **80**
      flour-coated, meat and skin   **120**
      batter-dipped or breaded, meat
        and skin   **195**
    thigh, one medium
      meat only   **110**
      flour-coated, meat and skin   **160**
      batter-dipped or breaded, meat
        and skin   **235**

Chicken-Continued
  roasted
    breast half, one medium
      meat only   **140**
      meat and skin   **190**
    drumstick, one medium
      meat only   **75**
      meat and skin   **110**

Turkey, roasted, 3 ounces
  (three slices 3 x 2 x ¼ inches)
    light meat only   **135**
    light meat and skin   **165**
    dark meat only   **160**
    dark meat and skin   **185**

Fish and Shellfish Calories

Clams, canned, drained, 3 ounces (about five to nine medium) — **80**

Crabmeat, canned or cooked, 3 ounces (about 2/3 cup) — **85**

Cod, breaded, fried, 3 ounces — **180**

Fish, battered, fried, 3 ounces — **185**

Fish sticks, frozen, reheated, three — **175**

Flounder, baked or broiled, 3 ounces — **115**

Haddock, baked or broiled, 3 ounces — **110**

Fish and Shellfish-Continued   Calories

Ocean perch, breaded, fried, 3 ounces   **190**

Oysters, breaded, fried, large, three   **155**

Salmon, 3 ounces
  baked or broiled, red (piece 3 x 1¾
    x 1 inches)   **145**
  canned, drained (about ½ cup)   **125**

Sardines, Atlantic, canned in oil, drained,
  3 ounces (about seven medium)   **175**

Shrimp, 3 ounces
  canned (about 27 medium)   **100**
  french-fried, five large or eight medium   **210**

Tuna, chunk light, drained, 3 ounces
(about ½ cup)

canned in oil	**170**
canned in water	**110**

Eggs   Calories

Deviled, one large   **125**

Fried, one large   **95**

Hard or soft cooked, one large   **80**

Omelet, plain, one large egg, milk and
fat added   **105**

Poached, one large   **80**

Scrambled in fat, one large, milk added **105**

Dry Beans and Peas   Calories
*(For bean mixtures, see Mixed Dishes,
page 69.)*

Baked beans, canned, ½ cup
  with pork and tomato sauce   **155**
  with pork and sweet sauce   **140**

Black-eyed peas, cooked, drained, ½ cup **95**

Chickpeas (garbanzos), cooked, drained,
  ½ cup   **150**

Dry Beans and Peas-Continued   Calories

Lima, cooked, drained, ½ cup   **105**

Pinto, cooked, drained, ½ cup   **95**

Red kidney, canned with liquid, ½ cup   **110**

White (Navy (pea), Great Northern),
   cooked, drained, ½ cup   **120**

Nuts and Seeds   Calories

Almonds, 1 ounce (about 22)   **165**

Cashews, dry-roasted or oil-roasted,
   1 ounce (about 18)   **160**

Coconut, dried, sweetened, flaked,
2 tablespoons **45**

Mixed nuts, with peanuts, 1 ounce (about
20 assorted)
dry-roasted **165**
oil-roasted **175**

Peanuts, dry-roasted or oil-roasted,
1 ounce (about 28 whole) **165**

Peanut butter, 2 tablespoons **190**

Pecans, 1 ounce (about 20 halves) **185**

Pistachio nuts, dry-roasted, 1 ounce
(about 47) **170**

Sesame seeds, 1 tablespoon **50**

Sunflower seeds, roasted, hulled,
  2 tablespoons   **105**

Walnuts
  black, chopped, 1 ounce (about ¼ cup)   **170**
  English, 1 ounce (about 14 halves)   **180**

MILK, YOGURT, AND CHEESE

Fluid Milk   Calories

Buttermilk, 1 cup   **100**

Lowfat, no milk solids added, 1 cup
  1% fat   **105**
  2% fat   **120**

Skim, no milk solids added, 1 cup   **85**

Whole, 1 cup   **150**

Canned Milk   Calories

Condensed, sweetened, undiluted,
½ cup   **490**
Evaporated, undiluted, ½ cup
whole   **170**
skim   **100**

Milk Beverages   Calories

Chocolate milk, 1 cup
2% fat   **180**
whole   **210**

Eggnog, plain, commercial, 1 cup   **345**

Malted milk, prepared from powder with
   whole milk, 1 cup

natural	**210**
chocolate-flavored	**200**

Thick shake, commercially prepared,
   10 fluid ounces

chocolate	**360**
vanilla	**355**

Yogurt   Calories

Made from lowfat milk, with added nonfat
   milk solids
      8-ounce container

plain	**145**
flavored	**195**
fruit varieties	**230**

      6-ounce container

flavored	**145**
fruit varieties	**175**

Made from skim milk, with added
nonfat milk solids, plain,
8-ounce container   **125**

Made from whole milk
8-ounce container
  plain   **140**
  flavored   **230**
  fruit varieties   **270**
6-ounce container
  flavored   **170**
  fruit varieties   **200**

Cheese

Calories

American
process
1-ounce slice	105
1-inch cube	65
shredded, ½ cup (2 ounces)	210

process cheese food
1-ounce slice	90
1-inch cube	55
1 tablespoon	50

process cheese spread, 1 tablespoon   45

Blue, crumbled, ¼ cup   120

Brick
1-ounce slice	105
1-inch cube	65

Cheddar
1 ounce	115
1-inch cube	70
shredded, ½ cup (2 ounces)	225

Colby
   1-ounce slice   **110**
   1-inch cube   **70**

Cottage cheese, ½ cup
   creamed (4% fat)   **110**
   lowfat (2% fat)   **100**
   dry curd (less than ½% fat)   **60**

Cream cheese
   1 ounce   **100**
   1-inch cube   **55**
   1 tablespoon   **50**

Edam or Gouda
   1 ounce   **100**
   1-inch cube   **60**

Feta, crumbled, ¼ cup   **90**

Mozzarella, made with whole milk or part skim milk (low moisture)

1 ounce	80
1-inch cube	50
shredded, ½ cup (2 ounces)	160

Muenster

1 ounce	105
1-inch cube	65

Parmesan, grated, 1 tablespoon   25

Provolone

1-ounce slice	100
1-inch cube	60

Swiss, natural

1-ounce slice	105
1-inch cube	55
shredded, ½ cup (2 ounces)	210

Cheese-Continued   Calories

Swiss, process
  1-ounce slice   **95**
  1-inch cube   **60**
  shredded, ½ cup (2 ounces)   **185**

MIXED DISHES AND FAST FOOD ENTREES

Mixed Dishes   Calories

Bean salad, sweet-sour dressing, ½ cup   **70**

Beef and vegetable stew, 1 cup   **175**

Mixed Dishes-Continued   Calories

Chili with beans, 1 cup   **305**

Egg roll, with meat, one   **120**

Fried rice, with meat, 1 cup   **290**

Lasagna, piece 2½ x 4 inches, ⅙ of
   8-inch square   **330**

Macaroni and cheese, 1 cup   **515**

Potpie, frozen, baked, 8 ounces
   beef   **540**
   chicken   **495**

Mixed Dishes-Continued   Calories

Quiche lorraine, 1/8 of 8-inch quiche   **470**

Spaghetti in tomato sauce with cheese,
  1 cup   **155**

**Spaghetti with meat sauce or meat
  balls and tomato sauce**, 1 cup   **310**

Fast Food Entrees   Calories

Breakfast sandwich (egg, cheese,
  canadian bacon, english muffin), one   **385**

Cheeseburger, with catsup, mustard,
lettuce, tomatoes, pickles, and/or onions
    2-ounce patty (before cooking)   **360**
    4-ounce patty (before cooking)   **565**

Chicken, fried (see Poultry, page 54)

Enchilada, with beef and cheese, one   **325**

Fish sandwich with 1¾-ounce fried fish
fillet, tartar sauce, and cheese   **525**

Hamburger sandwich with catsup, mustard,
lettuce, tomatoes, pickles, and/or onions
    2-ounce patty (before cooking)   **280**
    4-ounce patty (before cooking)   **510**
    double meat patty   **540**

Pizza, 1/8 of 15-inch-diameter pizza
   cheese   **255**
   pepperoni   **325**

Roast beef sandwich, 2½ ounces meat,
   without condiments   **345**

Taco, meat, one
   small   **370**
   large   **570**

SOUPS

Canned Soups

(Canned, condensed, prepared with equal volume of water unless otherwise stated.)

Bean with bacon, 1 cup — **170**

Beef bouillon, broth, or consomme, 1 cup — **15**

Beef noodle, 1 cup — **85**

Chicken broth, 1 cup — **40**

Chicken noodle, 1 cup — **75**

Soups-Continued   Calories

Chicken rice, 1 cup   **60**

Clam chowder, 1 cup
  Manhattan-style   **80**
  New-England-style
    prepared with water   **95**
    prepared with skim milk   **130**
    prepared with whole milk   **165**

Cream of broccoli, 1 cup   **235**

Cream of chicken, 1 cup
  prepared with water   **115**
  prepared with skim milk   **160**
  prepared with whole milk   **190**

Cream of mushroom, 1 cup
  prepared with water   130
  prepared with skim milk   170
  prepared with whole milk   205

Minestrone, 1 cup   80

Pea, 1 cup
  green   165
  split, with ham   195

Tomato, 1 cup
  prepared with water   85
  prepared with skim milk   130
  prepared with whole milk   160

Vegetable, 1 cup
  with beef, chicken, or turkey   **80**
  vegetarian   **70**

Dehydrated Soups   Calories
*(One packet, prepared with 6 fluid ounces
of water.)*

Chicken noodle   **35**

Onion   **25**

Tomato vegetable   **55**

DESSERTS, SNACK FOODS, AND CANDY

Cakes

Calories

Angelfood cake, without frosting, 1/16 of 10-inch tube cake

145

Boston cream pie, 1/12 of 8-inch round cake

225

Carrot cake, with cream cheese frosting, 1/16 of tube cake

340

Cheesecake, 1/12 of 9-inch round cake **405**

Devil's-food or chocolate cake, with
  chocolate frosting, 1/16 of 8- or 9-inch
  round 2-layer cake   285

Fruitcake, dark, 1/32 of 7-inch round
  cake   165

Gingerbread, 1/9 of 8-inch square cake   240

Pound cake, without frosting, 1/16 of
  loaf 9 x 5 x 3 inches   220

Cupcakes, with frosting, 2¾-inch diameter
  chocolate   155
  not chocolate   170

Sponge cake, without frosting, 1/16 of
   10-inch tube cake   **145**

Yellow cake
   without frosting, 1/16 of bundt or
     tube cake   **190**
   with chocolate frosting, 1/16 of 8- or
     9-inch round 2-layer cake   **290**

Cookies and Bars   Calories

Brownie, with nuts, 2-inch square, one
   without frosting   **130**
   with frosting   **175**

Chocolate chip cookie, 2-inch diameter,
   one   **50**

Cookies and Bars-Continued	Calories

Fig bar, 1½-inch square, one **55**

Oatmeal cookie, with raisins, 2⅝-inch
diameter, one **60**

Peanut butter cookie, 2⅝-inch diameter,
one **80**

Sandwich cookie, chocolate or vanilla,
1½-inch diameter, one **55**

Shortbread cookie, 2-inch diameter, one **75**

Sugar cookie, 2½-inch diameter, one **70**

Vanilla wafer, 1¾-inch diameter, one   **20**

Pies   Calories

One-crust pies, 1/8 of 9-inch pie
   Chocolate cream   **405**
   Custard   **285**
   Lemon meringue   **340**
   Pecan   **485**
   Pumpkin   **330**
   Strawberry   **385**

Two-crust pies, 1/8 of 9-inch pie
   Apple   **455**
   Blueberry   **410**
   Cherry or peach   **405**

Fried pies
Apple   **310**
Cherry   **285**

Milk-Based Desserts   Calories

Custard, baked, ½ cup   **130**

Ice cream, ½ cup
regular (about 10% fat)   **135**
rich (about 16% fat)   **175**

Ice milk, ½ cup
hardened   **95**
soft serve   **115**

Puddings, ½ cup
(Prepared from mix with whole milk; puddings
   prepared with skim milk are about 30
   calories less per ½-cup serving.)

	Calories
chocolate	
instant	**160**
regular	**160**
chocolate mousse	**190**
rice	**160**
tapioca	**130**
vanilla	
instant	**150**
regular	**140**

Sherbet, ½ cup   **135**

Yogurt, frozen, ½ cup   **105**

Other Desserts

Calories

Fruit juice bars, frozen, 2½ fluid ounces **70**

Gelatin dessert, prepared, plain, ½ cup **70**

Popsicle, 3-fluid-ounce size **70**

Snack Foods

Calories

Cheese curls or puffs
10 pieces **85**
1-ounce package **160**

Corn chips
10 chips **95**
1-ounce package **150**

Crackers (see Crackers, page 27)

Nuts (see Nuts and Seeds, page 60)

Popcorn, 1 cup
air-popped   **30**
popped in vegetable oil   **65**

Pork rinds, deep-fried, 1 ounce (about
  1 cup)   **150**

Potato chips, regular
10 chips   **105**
1-ounce package   **145**

Pretzels
Dutch, twisted, 2¾ x 2⅝ inches, one   **60**
Soft, twisted, one   **190**
Stick, 2½ inches long, 10   **20**
Thin, twisted, 3¼ x 2¼ x ¼ inches,
  five   **115**

Candy   Calories

Caramels, 1 ounce (about three pieces)
chocolate   **85**
plain   **110**
tootsie roll, 1¼-ounce roll   **140**

Chocolate, sweetened
  candy-coated, 10 pieces
     plain   35
     with peanut butter   35
     with nuts   100
  milk (about 1½-ounce bar)
     plain   245
     with almonds   235
     with rice cereal   215
     with peanuts (1¾-ounce bar)   280
  semisweet chips, ¼ cup   215

Fondant, 10 pieces
  uncoated
     candy corn   35
     mints, pastel (about ⅝-inch square)   75
  chocolate-coated
     miniature mints   95

Fruit leather, 1 ounce   **80**

Fudge, vanilla or chocolate, 1 ounce
  plain   **110**
  with nuts   **120**

Granola bar (about 1½ ounces), one
  oats, raisins, coconut   **195**
  oats, peanuts, wheat germ   **205**

Gum drops, 1 ounce (about 8 pieces)   **95**

Hard candy, 1 ounce (about 5 pieces or
2 lollipops)   **105**

Jelly beans, 1 ounce (10 pieces about
  ¾ x ½ inch)   **95**

Licorice
  bite size, ¼ cup   **170**
  stick, 6½ inches long, one   **40**
  shoestring, 43 inches long, one   **70**

Marshmallows, 1 ounce (about 1⅛-inch
  diameter), about four   **90**

BEVERAGES
(Milk beverages and juices are in the Milk, Vegetable, and Fruit sections.)

Fruit Drinks

Calories

Fruit-flavored drink, prepared from
  powder, 8 fluid ounces
    presweetened
      regular   120
      low calorie   5
    sugar added   90

Fruit drinks, canned, 8 fluid ounces
  fruit punch   115
  grape or orange   125

Lemonade or limeade, frozen
  concentrate, sweetened, reconstituted,
  8 fluid ounces   **100**

Carbonated Beverages   Calories

Club soda, 12-ounce can   **0**

Cola-type, 12-ounce can
  regular   **150**
  diet   **5**

Fruit-flavored, 12-ounce can
  regular   **150**
  diet   **0**

Carbonated Beverages-Continued   Calories

Ginger ale, 12-ounce can
   regular   **125**
   diet   **0**

Root beer, 12-ounce can
   regular   **150**
   diet   **0**

Coffee and Tea   Calories

Coffee and tea, brewed or instant,
   unsweetened, 6-fluid-ounce cup   **Trace**

Tea, instant, presweetened mix,
  8 fluid ounces
    regular   **25**
    low calorie   **5**

Alcoholic Beverages   Calories

Beer, 12-ounce can or bottle
  regular   **150**
  light   **100**

Gin, rum, vodka, scotch, or bourbon,
  1½-fluid-ounce jigger   **105**

Wines
  table, red or white, 5-fluid-ounce glass   **100**
  dessert, 3½-fluid-ounce glass   **155**
  coolers, 8-fluid-ounce glass   **120**

SUGARS, SYRUPS, JAMS, AND JELLIES

Calories

Chocolate syrup, 1 tablespoon
 thin type   **40**
 fudge type   **70**

Honey, 1 tablespoon   **65**

Jams and preserves, 1 tablespoon   **55**

Jellies, 1 tablespoon   **50**

Sugar, granulated or brown, 1 tablespoon   **50**

Table syrup, 1 tablespoon   **55**

FATS, OILS, AND CREAMS

Fats and Oils
Calories

Butter or stick margarine
    1 teaspoon or 1 pat   **35**
    1 tablespoon   **100**

Margarine, soft, 1 teaspoon
    regular   **35**
    diet   **15**

Table spread, 1 teaspoon   **25**

Oil, 1 tablespoon   **120**

Salad dressings, commercial, 1 tablespoon
  regular
    blue or Roquefort cheese   **75**
    buttermilk   **55**
    creamy-type   **70**
    french   **65**
    italian   **70**
    mayonnaise   **100**
    mayonnaise-type   **55**
    russian   **75**
    thousand island   **60**
  low-calorie
    french   **20**
    italian   **15**
    mayonnaise   **35**
    mayonnaise-type   **35**
    thousand island   **25**

Cream

Calories

Half-and-half (milk and cream),
  1 tablespoon — **20**

Light, coffee or table, 1 tablespoon — **30**

Sour, 1 tablespoon — **30**

Whipped, pressurized, 2 tablespoons — **20**

Whipping, heavy
  unwhipped, 1 tablespoon — **50**
  whipped, 2 tablespoons — **50**

Imitation Cream Products   Calories
(Made with vegetable fat.)

Creamers
liquid, 1 tablespoon   **20**
powdered, 1 teaspoon   **10**

Sour dressing (nonbutterfat sour cream),
1 tablespoon   **25**

Whipped dessert topping, 2 tablespoons
frozen   **30**
powdered, made with whole milk   **20**
pressurized   **25**

CONDIMENTS

Barbecue sauce, 1 tablespoon — 10

Catsup, 1 tablespoon — 20

Gravy, 2 tablespoons
meat or poultry — 20
mushroom — 10

Horseradish, 1 tablespoon — 5

Mustard, prepared, yellow, 1 teaspoon — 5

Olives, canned
   green, stuffed or with pits, four small or
     three large   **15**
   ripe, mission, pitted, three medium or
     two extra large   **15**

Pickles
   dill, 3¾ inches long, one   **5**
   sweet gherkin, about 2½ inches long,
     one   **20**

Relish, sweet, finely chopped,
  1 tablespoon   **20**

Soy sauce, 1 tablespoon   **10**

Steak sauce, 1 tablespoon   **10**

Tartar sauce, 1 tablespoon   **75**

Serving Sizes of Meat

Calorie counts for many meat and poultry items in the Calorie Table are for 3 ounces of cooked meat. Many people have difficulty judging how their servings compare with a 3-ounce serving.

The sketches on the following pages can help to estimate serving sizes of meats. The sketch of the hamburger patty represents the approximate size and thickness of a 3-ounce serving. Two slices of meat or three slices of poultry of the size and thickness shown equal about 3 ounces. If your serving is larger or smaller, thicker or thinner, than the serving pictured, adjust the number of calories accordingly.

Hamburger

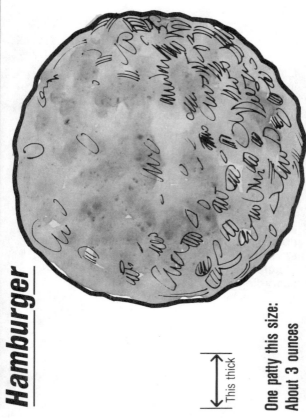

This thick

One patty this size:
About 3 ounces

Meat

Two slices this size: About 3 ounces

↕ This thick

Poultry

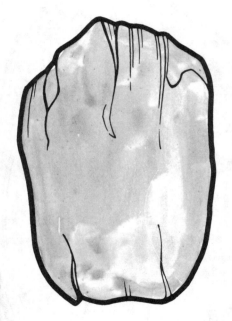

This thick

Three slices this size: About 3 ounces

Index to the Calorie Table

Foods are listed alphabetically under the food group in the Calorie Table.

Index to the Calorie Table-Continued

Index to the Calorie Table-Continued

Index to the Calorie Table-Continued

Index to the Calorie Table-Continued

Index to the Calorie Table-Continued

For More Information

- Contact your local county Extension agent, public health nutritionist, or dietitian in hospitals or other community agencies.

- Look through cookbooks in your local library for low-calorie recipes. Evaluate the recipes on the basis of what you have read here about weight control and the calories and nutrients provided by food.

- Contact the Human Nutrition Information Service (HNIS) for information on the Dietary Guidelines and other current publications about food, nutrition, and health. The address is U.S. Department of Agriculture, HNIS, Room 325-A, 6505 Belcrest Road, Hyattsville, Maryland 20782.